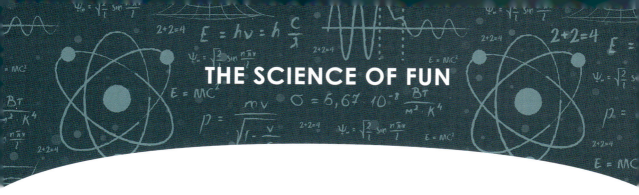

THE SCIENCE OF FUN

THE SCIENCE OF PLAYGROUNDS

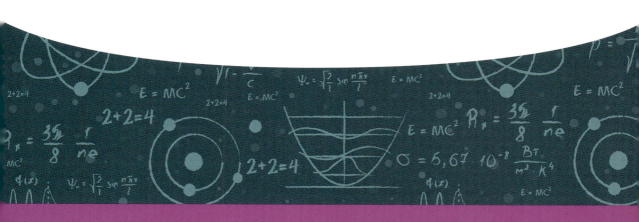

BY R. L. VAN

CONTENT CONSULTANT
Katie Hinko, PhD
Assistant Professor, Lyman Briggs College & P-A
Physics Education & Outreach
Michigan State University

Cover image: Gravity and other forces are at work when someone swings.

An Imprint of Abdo Publishing
abdobooks.com

abdobooks.com

Published by Abdo Publishing, a division of ABDO, PO Box 398166, Minneapolis, Minnesota 55439. Copyright © 2022 by Abdo Consulting Group, Inc. International copyrights reserved in all countries. No part of this book may be reproduced in any form without written permission from the publisher. Core Library™ is a trademark and logo of Abdo Publishing.

Printed in the United States of America, North Mankato, Minnesota
052021
092021

Cover Photo: Karel Noppe/iStockphoto
Interior Photos: iStockphoto, 4–5, 19, 24–25, 27, 29, 32, 34–35, 39, 43, 45; Ron and Patty Thomas/iStockphoto, 6; Monkey Business Images/iStockphoto, 8; Joe Prachatree/Shutterstock Images, 11; Anurak Pongpatimet/Shutterstock Images, 14–15; Shutterstock Images, 17; Necete da me Prevarite/Shutterstock Images, 22 (left person and swing frame); Cristopher Orange/Shutterstock Images, 22 (right person); PeopleImages/iStockphoto, 30

Editor: Marie Pearson
Series Designer: Katharine Hale

Library of Congress Control Number: 2020948173

Publisher's Cataloging-in-Publication Data

Names: Van, R. L., author.
Title: The science of playgrounds / by R. L. Van
Description: Minneapolis, Minnesota : Abdo Publishing, 2022 | Series: The science of fun | Includes online resources and index.
Identifiers: ISBN 9781532195181 (lib. bdg.) | ISBN 9781644946121 (pbk.) | ISBN 9781098215491 (ebook)
Subjects: LCSH: Playgrounds--Juvenile literature. | Force and energy--Juvenile literature. | Physics--Juvenile literature. | Dynamics--Juvenile literature. | Motion--Juvenile literature.
Classification: DDC 531.1--dc23

CONTENTS

CHAPTER ONE
Let It Slide 4

CHAPTER TWO
In Full Swing 14

CHAPTER THREE
Spinning Science 24

CHAPTER FOUR
Ups and Downs 34

Fast Facts 42

Stop and Think 44

Glossary 46

Online Resources 47

Learn More 47

Index 48

About the Author 48

CHAPTER
ONE

LET IT SLIDE

Jayden and Emily can't wait for recess. After lunch, they rush outside. They go straight to the playground. The two friends go down the slides every day they can. They feel like they're flying as they glide down to the ground.

Emily climbs the steps to their favorite slide. It's the yellow one that spirals around in a corkscrew. Jayden follows close behind.

Science helps make playgrounds fun and safe.

The type of slide will change the way gravity moves the person down it.

The top of the slide is a flat surface. It's covered by a plastic roof. There's a bar to hold on to. Emily uses the bar to get in position. She sits at the top and inches over the edge. Then she lets go of the bar and puts her hands on the sides of the slide. She pushes off. She takes the first turn slowly. But she starts to go faster as she swirls down the slide. She's going fast enough that she feels like she could fly off the end!

When Emily's ride is over, she climbs off and waits for Jayden. He comes speeding down the slide after her. They rush to get back in line for another turn.

DOWNWARD SLIDE

Playgrounds can be different from each other. But just about every playground has a slide. Some twist around. Some follow straight paths to the ground. No matter what type of slide a person goes down,

THE IMPORTANCE OF PLAY

Some kids don't have access to playgrounds at their schools or in their communities. But it's important for all kids to have safe playgrounds available. Playgrounds can have many benefits for kids. Students at an elementary school in Texas get multiple recesses a day. This is because studies have shown that kids learn better after breaks for playing and moving. It makes the students healthier. Playgrounds also help with physical and mental growth. Playground equipment can help kids develop their strength and other skills. Interaction with other kids on the playground helps them with their social skills too.

certain forces will act on that person. Forces are pushes and pulls on an object. Two main forces that act on people going down slides are gravity and friction.

Gravity is a force that pulls everything toward Earth's center. When people jump up, they fall back to the ground because of gravity. Gravity is always acting on objects, including people. When a girl is on the flat surface at the top of a slide, gravity pulls her toward the ground. But the surface beneath her keeps her from falling. When she moves forward, the surface beneath her changes. It is sloped. This means the surface isn't flat. It is slanted toward the ground.

When the girl is on the slide, the sloped surface doesn't push back up on the girl as much as the flat surface did. So gravity pulls her toward the ground. It moves her down the slide. The steeper the slide, the more quickly gravity can pull her down.

It is safest to go down a slide feetfirst.

Another main force acting on sliders is friction. Friction is a force between two objects rubbing together. It makes the objects stick together. This is because there are tiny bumps and grooves on surfaces. They are even on surfaces that seem smooth, such as a slide. These bumps and grooves catch against each other. They create a force that resists motion. Friction between sliders and a slide slows the people down as they go down the slide.

There are some ways to lower the amount of friction between a person and the slide. One is wearing clothing that moves easily against the slide's surface. Going down a slide in shorts in the summer can hurt the skin on a person's legs. That is because there is a lot of friction between skin and the material the slide is made of. But going down a slide in sweatpants doesn't hurt. The fabric has little friction with the slide. This lets the person move down the slide more quickly.

Slides come in many shapes and sizes. But the forces that make slides work are the same.

> **NEW HEIGHTS**
>
> Playground slides aren't usually very tall. But one slide in London, England, is 584 feet (178 m) long. It's the world's tallest, longest, and fastest tunnel slide. It wraps around a tall sculpture at a park in London. Parts of the tunnel are clear. Riders can see through it while they speed down the slide. They can go up to 15 miles per hour (24 km/h). It takes 40 seconds to make it to the bottom.

Playgrounds are filled with fun equipment. There are slides, swings, monkey bars, and more. Playgrounds are made for kids to have fun. They're also great places to learn. Science is a part of everything kids do on playgrounds. It lets kids move quickly down slides and swing high in the air. Understanding the science behind playgrounds is just another way to have fun on them!

STRAIGHT TO THE
SOURCE

Expert in play and playgrounds Joe L. Frost talked about the benefits and drawbacks of common playground designs:

Playing in natural environments compliments the physical activities of playing in play yards. Children need opportunities to explore nature, and they need free, spontaneous play on physically challenging play spaces and equipment. . . . A playground builds skills in hanging from overhead [objects], swinging, running, sliding, chasing, throwing, catching, climbing, and playing traditional games. . . .

However, playgrounds built around this equipment had major problems—a lack of open spaces, natural features, found materials, and loose parts, all of which are so essential to children's creative, spontaneous play.

Source: "What's Wrong with America's Playgrounds and How to Fix Them." *American Journal of Play*, vol. 1, no. 2, Fall 2008, eric.ed.gov. Accessed 21 May 2020.

CONSIDER YOUR AUDIENCE

Adapt this passage for a different audience, such as your friends. Write a blog post conveying this information for the new audience. How does your post differ from the original text and why?

CHAPTER TWO

IN FULL SWING

Another popular playground activity is swinging. People on swings pump their legs to swing higher. They swing back and forth. Science is behind all of the movements and sensations of swinging.

Understanding the science behind swings is easier with an understanding about the laws of motion. Isaac Newton was an English scientist from the 1600s who helped write down these laws. The laws of motion describe how objects move. The first law states that an

Many people enjoy playing on swings.

15

object at rest, meaning an object that isn't moving, will stay at rest until a force acts on it to make it move. The first law of motion also states that a moving object will keep moving at the same speed in the same direction until a force acts on it to change its motion. An object's ability to keep moving at the same speed in the same direction or to stay at rest is called inertia. It is harder to change the motion of an object with more inertia than the motion of an object with less inertia.

SWING HISTORY

Swings have been around for thousands of years. In the 1800s, many people attached swings to trees. Playgrounds became more common in the early 1900s, and these spaces often featured swings. People were soon able to put swing sets in their backyards.

The design of swings has changed over time. Soft surfaces are built under today's swing sets. This helps to cushion falls. Some swings are made to be safer for very young children. And some swings are easy and safe for children with special needs to use. There are swings that can be ridden with a wheelchair.

Isaac Newton did experiments to understand motion and energy.

The first law of motion is at play on the swings. A boy sits still in a swing. He and the swing are at rest, so they will stay at rest until a force acts on them. He pushes backward off the ground with his feet. This push is the force that puts the swing in motion. After this push, inertia keeps the swing moving. Another force has to act on the swing to stop it from moving backward.

Swings are pendulums. Pendulums are objects hanging on the end of a rod or a string that swings freely. The top of the rod or string is attached to a point that doesn't move. When a pendulum starts moving, it picks up speed as gravity pulls it down. This is because of the first law of motion. But as the pendulum reaches its lowest point, the force of gravity slows it down. As the pendulum goes back up, it rises until gravity stops it completely. Then gravity pulls it back down.

After gravity pulls the boy and the swing downward, they keep moving. This is because they have enough inertia to move forward and upward, against the force of gravity. But the forces of friction slow a pendulum down. On a swing, there is friction from the air pushing against the boy and the swing itself. There is also friction where the chain is attached

The speed of a swing changes depending on its height above the ground.

SWINGING TOGETHER

Swinging with friends can be fun. But it can offer more than just entertainment. One study asked children to swing together. Some of the children were told to match their swinging to that of another child. They matched up their movements. Other children did not try to match each other's movements. Afterward, the children had to work together to complete a task. Those who had matched their movements communicated better to complete the task than children who hadn't.

to the swing set. People on swings pump their legs or are pushed to keep friction from stopping their movement. This adds energy to their swinging.

ENERGY AND SWINGS

Energy is the ability something has to do work, meaning to move something against a force. There are two main types of energy. One is potential energy. This energy is stored in an object. The other type of energy is kinetic energy. This is the energy of something that is moving.

A girl stands in front of a swing. She holds the chains in her hands and backs up as far as she can. The swing lifts into the air. This creates potential energy. There is energy stored in the girl and in the swing. This includes gravitational potential energy, which is the potential energy something has when gravity is working to pull it downward. When the girl lifts her feet off the ground and sits in the swing, that potential energy becomes kinetic energy. The swing moves forward. It follows an arced path. That path is shaped like a U. While the swing moves through the lowest part of the arc, its kinetic energy is highest because it is moving the fastest. When it is on the ends of the arc and higher in the air, the swing's potential energy is highest. As the girl swings, the energy changes from potential energy to kinetic energy and back again.

    The girl pumps her legs as she swings back and forth. This action changes her center of mass, which is balanced around her at any moment. She swings forward. At the top of the forward arc of her swing,

ENERGY IN SWINGING

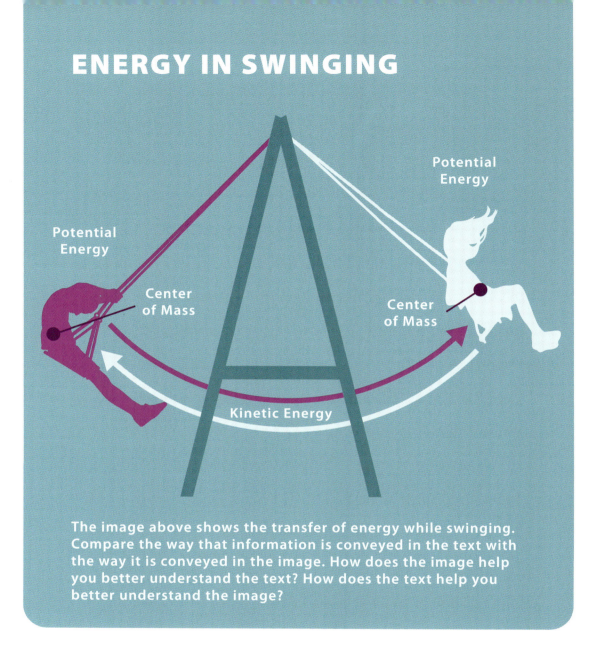

The image above shows the transfer of energy while swinging. Compare the way that information is conveyed in the text with the way it is conveyed in the image. How does the image help you better understand the text? How does the text help you better understand the image?

she tucks her legs under her. She leans forward slightly. This causes her center of mass to be even higher. She has more potential energy for swinging backward.

That potential energy then changes to kinetic energy as the swing moves back down. She moves backward faster, and she reaches that same height on the backward swing. Then she leans backward and straightens her legs. This helps move her center of mass higher at the top of the backward arc. Once again, the girl can get higher and add more potential energy. She can keep swinging as long as she uses her body to add more energy to her motion.

EXPLORE ONLINE

Chapter Two discusses some of the science behind swinging. The article at the website below has more information on this topic. What information does the website give about the science of swinging? What other information does it cover? How is the information at the website similar to the information in Chapter Two? What new information did you learn from the website?

WHEN WERE SWINGS INVENTED?

abdocorelibrary.com/science-playgrounds

CHAPTER
THREE

SPINNING SCIENCE

Playgrounds are full of objects that spin or move in circles. Different forces are at work in these playground toys. One common playground toy is the tetherball. This is a pole with a string attached to the top. At the other end of the string is a ball. When someone hits this ball, it moves away from the pole. The string stretches tight. The string exerts tension force on the ball. Tension force is the pulling force of a rope or string on another object.

Parks and playgrounds can be great places to spend time with family.

25

TETHERBALL IN SPACE

In a game of tetherball, a string connects the ball to the pole. This is what makes it move in a circle. Planets in the solar system travel around the sun. But there is no string connecting Earth to the sun. Gravity acts as a tether instead. The sun is so large that it exerts a lot of gravitational pull on the planets around it. This pulls the planets toward the sun, just like a string pulls a tetherball toward the pole. The sun's gravity creates the centripetal force to keep planets in orbit, moving in a curved path around the sun.

In tetherball, the ball starts moving at a certain speed in the direction in which it was hit. This is the ball's velocity, meaning its speed in a straight line. The first law of motion states that an object in motion will continue moving at the same velocity until another force acts on it. So the ball attempts to move in a straight line. But the string connecting the ball to the pole stops it from doing this. Its tension force pulls the ball inward, toward the pole in the center. This inward,

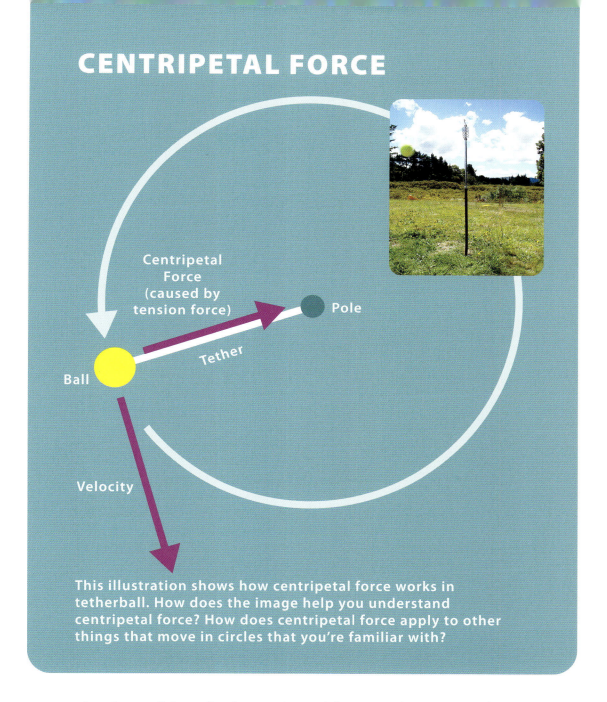

This illustration shows how centripetal force works in tetherball. How does the image help you understand centripetal force? How does centripetal force apply to other things that move in circles that you're familiar with?

circular pull is called centripetal force. It keeps an object moving in a circle.

MERRY-GO-ROUNDS

Playground merry-go-rounds are a little different from an amusement park carousel. A merry-go-round at a playground is a big circular platform, or disk. The disk spins around a post in the center. There are bars attached to the top of the disk. Riders hold on to the bars while they spin around on the disk.

A merry-go-round starts out sitting still. To make a merry-go-round move, someone has to give it a push. The first law of motion says that an object in motion will keep moving in the same direction until a force acts on it. But a boy sitting on a merry-go-round doesn't keep moving in the direction of the push. He moves in a circle. This is because his grip on the bars creates centripetal force. It keeps him rotating at the same distance from the center of the merry-go-round.

The spot on the merry-go-round where the boy is sitting will affect the centripetal force acting on him. If he is on the outside of the circle, he is moving a greater

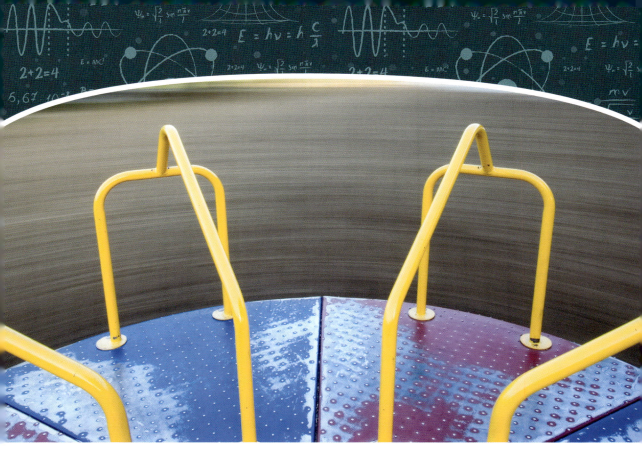

The center of a merry-go-round moves slower than the outside edges.

distance to go all the way around. Someone sitting in the center moves a much shorter distance to make a full rotation around the pole. The boy on the outside is moving faster. He is also getting dizzier.

Dizziness is caused by effects on the inner ear. The inner ear is inside the head. Three tubes in the inner ear help with keeping balance. Each one has liquid and tiny

Getting dizzy makes it difficult to stay balanced.

hairs inside. When a person moves his or her head, it makes the liquid in these tubes move. The liquid then moves the hairs. This tells the brain how the person is moving.

A girl on the merry-go-round begins to spin. The liquid in her inner ears sloshes backward. It pushes the tiny hairs back. The brain senses her moving. But as she spins around and around, the liquid adjusts. It moves the same way the girl is moving. The hairs straighten out again. Her brain doesn't sense movement anymore.

When the girl gets off the ride, she stops moving. But the liquid in her inner ear has inertia. It keeps moving in the direction in which she was spinning.

SENSATIONAL SPINNING

Getting dizzy might seem like just a silly way to have fun. But it's also a way children develop their vestibular system. This is the system in the inner ear that senses the body's position. It provides a person's sense of balance. The vestibular sense can also affect posture and coordination. Playground activities including swinging and going down slides help develop this system. So do rides that involve spinning, such as merry-go-rounds and other playground spinners. Playing on a playground can have some important benefits!

Some people enjoy getting a little dizzy on a merry-go-round.

This pushes the hairs and sends a message to her brain that she's moving even though she's not. This causes the dizzy feeling.

STRAIGHT TO THE
SOURCE

Shane's Inspiration is an organization that designs playgrounds accessible to children with disabilities. Employee Diane Scanlan spoke about the importance of the work:

> *Inclusive design has forced designers to be more creative. No longer are we providing the simple function of a swing or slide but designing an environment with multi-sensory experiences. . . . I learn from watching kids interact with play equipment. I come away with information: why is it working for them, why is it not, how can we make it a more sensory experience? . . . That's how a roller slide turned into a roller table: someone let us know that a child with a disability was fearful of being put on their back and going down the slide. If one piece of equipment isn't working for one set of needs, then we choose to adapt it.*
>
> Source: "Changing Perceptions, Transforming Play." *Playground Professionals*, 19 Mar. 2018, playgroundprofessionals.com. Accessed 22 May 2020.

WHAT'S THE BIG IDEA?

Read the passage above closely. What connection is being made between playground design and inclusion? Write down two or three details from the passage that support this main idea.

CHAPTER
FOUR

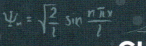

UPS AND DOWNS

Part of the fun of playgrounds is moving up and down. Playgrounds offer kids an opportunity to climb that they might not have anywhere else. Monkey bars and seesaws are popular parts of playgrounds.

ON THE MONKEY BARS

Many playgrounds feature monkey bars. Climbing monkey bars requires using a lot of different skeletal muscles. These are the

Many muscles are at work to keep balance and climb on playground equipment.

muscles in the human body that people use for most movement. When people want to move their legs, their brains signal certain muscles in the legs. The fibers in these muscles lengthen or shorten. This creates the forces for movement.

    A girl reaches her arms up to grab the monkey bars. Muscles in her shoulders, arms, and back lengthen and shorten to help her do this. Then she has to grab on to a bar. This requires a strong grip. The muscles in her hands and forearms work together. They move her hands and fingers so they wrap around the bar and hold tight. When her body is hanging above the ground, it has potential energy from gravity. Her hands have to hold her weight up, or she will fall down. This makes her muscles get stronger.

    Swinging on the monkey bars strengthens upper body muscles, including arm and shoulder muscles. It develops core muscles too. These are the muscles around the stomach and back. Core muscles are important for good posture and protecting the spine. Core muscles work to keep the body upright instead of swinging too far to the left or right. People often tuck their legs as they swing across the monkey bars. This also helps strengthen core muscles. Core muscles have to work to hold the legs in the tucked position.

Friction also helps the girl keep her grip on the bars. The more friction between the bar and the girl's hands, the easier it will be to hold on. If the girl's hands get sweaty, the sweat will reduce friction. Her hands will slide more

MONKEYING AROUND

Monkey bars are named because a person swings across monkey bars a lot like a monkey or ape swings from tree to tree. Apes have developed shoulders that are pushed out to the sides of their bodies. Their shoulder blades are more on the back instead of the sides. This allows the shoulder joint to have a much wider range of motion than other animals. Humans have similar shoulder joints. In fact, humans and certain other primates are the only living things that can swing in this way.

easily against the bars. Even if her grasping muscles are very strong, she'll struggle to hold on without enough friction.

TEETER-TOTTERING

Playground seesaws, or teeter-totters, lift riders into the air and back down again. Gravity acts as a force on both riders, but the seesaw does work on one rider to lift the person above the ground. The amount of work done depends on both force and distance. The greater the distance, the less force is needed to do the same amount of work.

A girl and her younger brother are playing on a seesaw. The long, narrow board they're sitting on is angled toward the ground. The boy's side of the board is in the air. The girl's side is on the ground. The girl can be lifted up if the boy can come back to the ground. He wouldn't be able to pick her up if they were simply standing on the ground. It would require more force than he could produce. But the board spreads

The weight of a person lifts the friend on the other side of the seesaw.

out the girl's weight across a greater distance. The added distance means less force is required to lift the boy's sister.

A seesaw is a lever. Levers have three main parts. One part is the fulcrum. This is the balancing point in the middle of the seesaw. The other two parts of a lever are the effort arm and the resistance arm. Each side of a seesaw's board is an arm. The effort arm is the side where work is being done to lift the object. The resistance arm is the side where forces are acting against that work.

SCIENCE PLAYGROUNDS

Playgrounds are wonderful places to explore science. Some schools, cities, and organizations have created science playgrounds. One Massachusetts school has a playground with equipment that kids can use to apply science lessons. The New York Hall of Science has a playground with a giant lever, slides, spinners, and more. It's easy to play and learn at the same time.

On this seesaw, the boy's side is the effort arm. Gravity is pulling his body down toward the ground. This means that the other side of the seesaw is pushing up on the girl. The girl's side is the resistance arm. Gravity is also pulling the girl's body down. A smaller force spread across a long length of arm can be equal to or greater than a stronger force on a small length of arm. So if the boy is far enough away from the fulcrum of the seesaw, the force will be spread out across enough distance. The force pushing up will be big enough to lift his sister. Once the girl is higher in the air than her brother is, her side will become the effort arm. The length of each arm spreads the effort and resistance forces out over distances. This makes it possible for levers to lift enormous weights.

Every piece of equipment on a playground has science behind it. Learning about the science behind playgrounds can make it even more fun to slide, swing, climb, and seesaw. Playing on the playground is a great way to observe physics, engineering, biology, and more in action!

FURTHER EVIDENCE

Chapter Four discusses the science behind seesaws. What is one of the main points of that part of the chapter? What evidence is included to support this point? Watch the video at the website below. Does the information in the video support the main point you identified? Does it present new evidence?

THE MIGHTY MATHEMATICS OF THE LEVER

abdocorelibrary.com/science-playgrounds

FAST FACTS

- The steepness of a slide affects how directly the force of gravity can act on a person sliding down it. The angled slide works against some of the force of gravity so that the person doesn't fall straight to the ground, but it still lets some gravity pull the person toward the ground.

- Friction makes objects stick together rather than slide easily against each other, so friction works to slow or stop movement.

- Swings work because of the inertia of a person on a swing. Inertia allows people to continue moving after gravity has already pulled them to the lowest point of the swing's path.

- People on swings use energy to increase their speed. They store energy from gravitational potential energy when up high. This turns into kinetic energy as they move through the swing's path, then turns back into gravitational potential energy as they go up higher in the air.

- Swinging across monkey bars uses muscles in the arms, shoulders, back, and core.

- Objects that spin or move in circles on a playground do so because of centripetal force.

- Spinning and moving in circles makes people dizzy because liquid in their ears moves along with their spinning movement. When a person stops, the liquid's inertia makes it keep moving, telling the brain that the person is spinning even when sitting still.

- A seesaw is a lever. It allows people to lift weights on the other side, such as another person they are playing with, when they otherwise could not. This is because the length of the seesaw's beam spreads the force out across a greater distance, which means it requires less force to lift the same weight.

STOP AND THINK

Tell the Tale

Chapter Three of this book discusses the science behind spinning on a merry-go-round. Imagine you are riding a merry-go-round at a playground. Write 200 words about your experience. What forces are acting on you? What sensations do these forces cause you to feel?

Surprise Me

Chapter Two discusses the science of playing on playground swings. After reading this book, what two or three facts about swinging did you find most surprising? Write a few sentences about each fact. Why did you find each fact surprising?

Dig Deeper

After reading this book, what questions do you still have about the science of playgrounds? With an adult's help, find a few reliable sources that can help you answer your questions. Write a paragraph about what you learned.

You Are There

New playgrounds are being designed and built all the time. Imagine you have been asked to design a new playground in your community. Make a list of the different kinds of equipment you would include. Think about where you would have the playground built. Then write a letter, as if you were going to send it to your local newspaper, explaining why you made these choices and how you think your decisions will help kids in your community.

GLOSSARY

center of mass
the point around which an object's mass is evenly spread

centripetal force
a force that acts on a moving object by pulling it around the center of something

energy
the ability something has to do work, which is defined as moving something against a force

exert
to put a force on something

force
a push or pull on an object that affects the way it moves

inertia
an object's tendency to continue moving in a straight line at the same speed or to stay at rest

lever
a simple machine that makes it easier to lift an object by spreading a smaller force over a greater distance on the other side

orbit
the path an object takes when moving around another object in space

skeletal muscle
a type of muscle that is connected to the bones of the skeleton and is used to move the skeleton

ONLINE RESOURCES

To learn more about the science of playgrounds, visit our free resource websites below.

Visit **abdocorelibrary.com** or scan this QR code for free Common Core resources for teachers and students, including vetted activities, multimedia, and booklinks, for deeper subject comprehension.

Visit **abdobooklinks.com** or scan this QR code for free additional online weblinks for further learning. These links are routinely monitored and updated to provide the most current information available.

LEARN MORE

Hustad, Douglas. *The Science of Amusement Parks.* Abdo Publishing, 2022.

Marquardt, Meg. *Physics in the Real World.* Abdo Publishing, 2016.

47

INDEX

apes, 37

centripetal force, 26–28

dizziness, 29, 31, 32

first law of motion, 15–18, 26, 28
friction, 9–10, 18–20, 37–38
Frost, Joe L., 13
fulcrum, 39–40

gravity, 9, 18, 21, 26, 36, 38, 40

inertia, 16, 18, 31
inner ear, 29–31

kinetic energy, 20–21, 22, 23

laws of motion, 15
levers, 39, 40, 41

merry-go-rounds, 28–32
monkey bars, 12, 35–38
muscles, 35–38

Newton, Isaac, 15

planets, 26
potential energy, 20–23, 36

Scanlan, Diane, 33
science playgrounds, 40
seesaws, 35, 38–41
Shane's Inspiration, 33
slides, 5–12, 31, 33, 40, 41
swings, 12, 13, 15, 16, 17–23, 31, 33, 41

tension force, 25–26, 27
tetherball, 25–27

velocity, 26, 27

About the Author

R. L. Van is a writer and editor living in the Twin Cities, Minnesota. She has written nonfiction books on a variety of subjects. In her free time, she enjoys reading, doing crossword puzzles, and caring for her pet cats.